GROWING UP IN THE EIGHTIES

Kathryn Walker

HODDER
Wayland

an imprint of Hodder Children's Books

Produced for Hodder Wayland by
Discovery Books Ltd
Unit 3, 37 Watling Street, Leintwardine, Shropshire SY7 0LW, England

First published in 2002 by Hodder Wayland, an imprint of Hodder Children's Books

British Library Cataloguing in Publication Data
Walker, Kathryn
Growing up in the eighties
1. Children - Great Britain - Social life and customs -
Juvenile literature 2. Nineteen eighties - Juvenile literature
3. Great Britain - Social conditions - 1945- - Juvenile literature
4. Great Britain - Social life and customs - 1945- - Juvenile literature
I. Title II. Eighties
941'. 0858' 0922

ISBN 0 7502 4088 1

Printed and bound by Grafiasa, Porto, Portugal

Designer: Ian Winton
Editor: Kathryn Walker

Hodder Children's Books would like to thank the following for the loan of their material:
Aquarius: cover (centre and right), page 16 © 1989 Grundy TV; **Corbis:** page 6 (bottom), 22 Annie
Griffiths, 24 (top); **Discovery Library:** page 7; **Duke of Edinburgh's Award:** page 11 (top left and
top right); **Ford:** page 24 (bottom); **Hulton Getty:** page 8 (top) Steve Eason; 25 (bottom); 28
(bottom), 29; **Last Resort Picture Library:** page 13 (bottom); **Motorola Archives:** page 23 (bottom
right); **Philips:** page 6 (top right and top left), 20, 23 (bottom left); **Porsche AG:** page 25 (top);
Redferns: page 18 (top), 21 (bottom); **Robert Opie:** page 10 (top), 12 (top), 13 (top), 14, 15, 17,
19 (bottom), 21 (top), 30; **Vodaphone Group:** page 23 (top right).

Hodder Children's Books
A division of Hodder Headline Limited
338 Euston Road
London NW1 3BH

CONTENTS

THE 1980s

The 1980s was a time when technology changed the way that people lived and worked. Computers rapidly became an important part of offices, schools and homes, and for those who had the money there were lots of other high-tech luxury goods to buy. But for some these were difficult times and in parts of Britain many jobs were lost.

Some now remember the eighties as a very selfish decade. It was certainly a time for showing off – the way things looked, and sometimes how much they cost, seemed very important. In this book four people tell us what it was like growing up in the 1980s.

REBECCA FORD
Rebecca Ford was born in 1975. She grew up with her two brothers in a town in Carmarthenshire, South Wales.

▶ Rebecca in 1985 aged 10.

EBRU GARNETT
Ebru Garnett was born in Sheffield in 1972 to parents of Turkish origin. She lived there with her parents and younger brother.

▶ Ebru in 1982 aged 10.

DARREN HUGGINS

Darren Huggins was born in Birmingham in 1973. He lived there with his grandparents, uncles and aunts throughout the eighties.

▶ Darren in 1982 aged 9.

JAMES KESSELL

James Kessell was born in 1971 in Nottingham. In 1979 his family moved to a town in West Sussex, where he lived with his younger brother and sister during the eighties.

▶ James in 1982 aged 11.

AT HOME

The number of electronic gadgets in the home was increasing. Video recorders (VCRs) had been around since the seventies, but in the eighties they became cheaper so more homes had one. New items appeared such as CD players, personal stereos, camcorders for making home videos and home computers.

Camcorders of the 1980s were much bigger than those of today.

A 1980s video recorder.

Games consoles that plugged into TV sets became very popular in the eighties.

James

In the early eighties I was given a Spectrum 48k computer for Christmas. I was able to write basic programs with it, but mostly I used it for playing games. It was the latest technology then, but by today's standards it was very, very basic.

RECYCLING

Throughout the seventies and eighties people looked for ways to reduce pollution and conserve natural resources. Saving certain kinds of household rubbish for recycling was something that everyone could do to help. Many recycling centres opened where people could take their old newspapers, bottles and cans.

HEALTH AND FITNESS

Now that so many families could drive everywhere, there were fears that people were generally not getting enough exercise. Adults and children were encouraged to take more care of their bodies. Exercise classes became very popular and so did fitness videos or audio tapes for exercising along with at home.

Leisure centres began to appear in many towns. People went to gyms and took up aerobics to help them stay healthy as well as look good. Some chose jogging as a way of keeping fit.

Darren

Sport was my life back in the eighties, so I was very fit. I did athletics, long distance running, cricket and played football at district and county levels. I'd also go jogging to keep fit, often listening to music on my personal stereo which seemed to help me set a pace.

At school in the eighties

In the eighties new school exams were introduced. In England and Wales the old GCE 'O' level and CSE exams for 16-year-olds were replaced by the GCSE. 'O' level pupils had been marked only on how well they did on examination day, but the GCSE allowed coursework to count as part of the total mark. This was seen as a fairer way of testing ability.

Primary and secondary schools began to use computers during the 1980s.

James

My 'O' levels were purely exam-based - there was no coursework and therefore no need to put in too much effort at school. It was quite possible to 'cram' between Easter and May. This suited some people (like me) but it didn't always test understanding. 'A' levels were a big step up from 'O' levels. However they were also exam-based and so meant a massive amount of cramming in the final weeks.

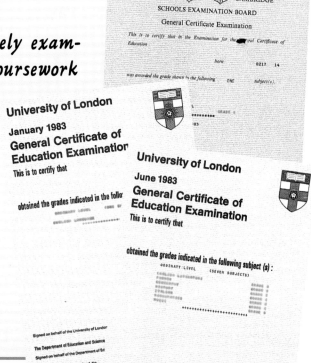

NATIONAL CURRICULUM

Before 1988 schools were free to choose most of the subjects they taught and how to teach them. In 1988 the National Curriculum was introduced, which told schools what to teach and how to test. This meant that throughout state schools in England and Wales children were learning many of the same subjects in the same way and at the same time.

CANING BANNED

In 1986 corporal punishment, which was physical punishment such as caning, was banned in state schools. Private schools, however, could continue to use it.

Rebecca

My younger brother sometimes got 'slippered' by the PE teacher and that was in a comprehensive school in 1988! The same teacher taught me maths. He was always shouting and I was so scared of him that sometimes I'd pretend to be ill to avoid going to his classes.

HAVING FUN

Now so many households had television, video and sophisticated 'hi-fi' systems there was plenty of entertainment to be had at home. The eighties was the decade of video games, and while some were played in arcades, there were many which could be played at home using units

Donkey Kong and Zelda were some of the many games programs of the 1980s.

that plugged into a TV set. In 1989 Nintendo brought out a small hand-held games unit called Game Boy which allowed people to play games anywhere.

But children still needed to get out of the house to do things and be with other children. The boy scouts and girl guides offered lots of activities and youth clubs gave young people somewhere to meet and organize their own entertainment.

Ebru

I didn't belong to any clubs, but I was one of a group of about 6 or 7 girlfriends and we spent all our spare time together in each other's houses.

Sometimes we'd all watch videos of our favourite programmes and we were always having sleep-overs.

Darren

I took part in the *Duke of Edinburgh's Award* scheme and got my bronze and silver certificates. One involved going on a canoeing expedition. After a week of training we'd meet once a week to plan our expedition. We had to map it out and work out how much we could carry - the expedition lasted 4-5 days, so we had to take camping equipment. Earning the certificate also involved helping people in the local community and we learnt a lot about dealing with people.

Silver

Bronze

Rebecca

I was with the brownies and girl guides between the ages of 7 and 14. One day someone from school made fun of me in my guides' uniform and after that I stopped going. Instead I started going to youth club once a week where we'd chat, play table tennis and sometimes organize outings.

OTHER TOYS AND CRAZES

The BMX, which appeared in the early eighties, was a sophisticated but expensive bike that could be used for stunt riding. A lot of children wanted one, particularly after it featured in the hit film *ET – The Extra-Terrestrial*. Skateboarding was a more affordable craze of the time. Top toys included Transformers, pictured here, which were toy robots that could be made into vehicles, and the Cabbage Patch Kid, which was a bit like an old-fashioned rag doll. But one of the strangest fads of the time that fascinated both adults and children was a puzzle called the Rubik's Cube.

Rebecca

As soon as I got my Cabbage Patch Kid I sent off for its birth certificate. Mine told me I was the mother of Nora, but I didn't like that name so I sent it back and had it changed to Belinda. A year later I received a card on Belinda's first birthday. I had quite a lot of dolls, and here's a picture of me on my birthday with one I got as a present.

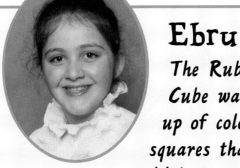

Ebru

The Rubik's Cube was made up of coloured squares that could be moved around and the aim was to get it so each side showed squares only of the same colour. I could only ever do one side, so I found out how to pull the Cube to bits and rebuild it when nobody was looking. They were a real craze - in school breaks everybody would start fiddling with their Cubes and hardly a word was spoken.

Eighties Fact
During the eighties over 200 million Rubik's Cubes were sold. A best-selling book on how to solve the Cube was written by a 12-year-old English boy, Patrick Bossert.

BMX bikes were well-suited to riding over rougher ground and BMX racing became a very popular sport in the 1980s.

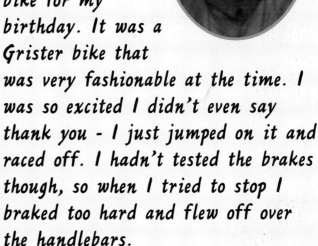

Darren

My dad bought me my first bike for my birthday. It was a Grister bike that was very fashionable at the time. I was so excited I didn't even say thank you - I just jumped on it and raced off. I hadn't tested the brakes though, so when I tried to stop I braked too hard and flew off over the handlebars.

FILMS

Many families could now hire films on video to watch at home so it wasn't surprising that fewer people were going to the cinema. But there were some hugely successful films of the time. Some used new computer technology to create thrilling special effects. The popular *Who Framed Roger Rabbit?* (1988) combined film of real actors with computer-generated cartoons.

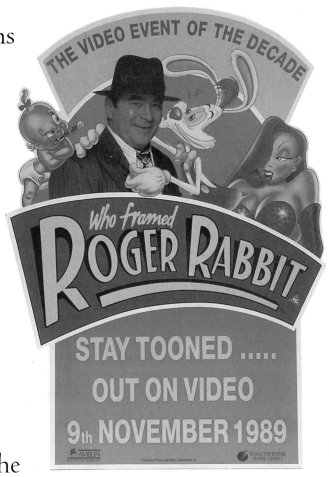

Fame (1980), was a film about ambitious American teenagers at the New York High School for Performing Arts. It sparked an energetic dance craze, a fashion for dance gear and a TV series. *Flashdance* (1983) was about a working girl trying to get herself a place at ballet school. Like *Fame*, it featured hit songs and spectacular dancing.

James

I went to see **Jaws III** in **3-D**. Everyone was given red and green coloured glasses to wear so that you got the **3-D** effect. The film wasn't very good, but the 3-D effects certainly made us scream when severed limbs came floating off the screen.

Ebru

*Films like **Fame** and **Flashdance** made modern dance very popular. **Flashdance** featured some breakdancing, which is very gymnastic. It really caught on, and groups of teenage boys would often turn up in our town centre, unroll linoleum pads, turn on their ghetto blasters and do some amazing breakdancing. Loads of people stopped to watch and cheer them. I thought they were really cool.*

One of the best-loved films of the decade was *ET – The Extra-Terrestrial* (1982). In it a loveable but rather ugly alien is trapped on Earth and befriends an American boy. Other successes of the time included the adventure film *Indiana Jones and the Temple of Doom, Gremlins* which had some cute little monsters and *Ghostbusters* (all 1984).

THEN & NOW

• In 1987-88, 84% of 7-14 year olds reported that they had visited the cinema. In 1998-99 this figure rose to 95%.

TELEVISION

The 1980s brought greater choice of TV viewing. In 1982 Channel 4 went on the air and in 1983 'breakfast TV' started. It meant people had a total of four channels to choose from, unless they had the latest satellite dish or cable TV which allowed them to pick up lots more.

For young children there were animations such as *Fireman Sam, Ivor the Engine* and *Thomas the Tank Engine*, which are still popular today. Realistic drama included *Grange Hill, Byker Grove* and the Australian series *Neighbours*, which although it had been aimed at adults became very popular with children.

Two of the actors in *Neighbours*, Jason Donovan and Kylie Minogue, went on to have careers as pop stars.

Rebecca

*At school we were always talking about **Neighbours**. At first it was shown at lunchtimes, but I think the **BBC** started showing it at tea-time because so many schoolkids liked to watch it. Jason Donovan and Kylie Minogue were having a romance both in the series and in real life. They made a hit single together called **Especially For You** which I bought.*

One of ITV's most successful shows of the time was *Spitting Image*. This was a programme of comic sketches using latex puppets that were caricatures of famous people, often politicians. The series carried on into the nineties.

Programmes 6-12 June 1987   35p
Thames/LWT and Channel Four
TV Times
87

THEN & NOW

• Children seem to be watching slightly less broadcast TV today than they did in the 1980s. In 1986 those aged between 4 and 15 were watching an average of 20 hours of TV per week. In 1999 the average viewing for the same age group was 18 hours per week.

Spitting Image puppets of leaders of the three main political parties in 1987.

Ebru

My friends and I loved watching **Blackadder**. *This was a comedy set in historical times with Rowan Atkinson playing the main character. We used to video it then go to each other's houses to watch it over and over again. We even used to learn the scripts by heart!*

Spitting Image *was another favourite. As the series progressed the puppet of Prime Minister Mrs Thatcher looked more and more like a man, so that in the end she wore a man's pinstripe suit and smoked a cigar.*

FASHION AND MUSIC

Sportswear such as tracksuits and trainers were very fashionable and suited the eighties' fitness craze. The film *Fame* started a trend for dancewear such as legwarmers, a kind of long, knitted tube worn over the lower leg. Some dressed up as pirates, dandies and other fantasy characters. They were known as 'new romantics'.

Shorter haircuts with long, floppy fringes, as worn here by pop band Duran Duran, were popular in the 1980s.

People also liked to dress in a way that made them look wealthy. Lots of girls copied the frilly-necked blouses and floral skirts worn by the young Princess Diana. Some young businesswomen wore expensive suits often with big padded shoulders. This became known as 'power dressing' because it made them look successful and businesslike.

James

I generally wore straight 'drainpipe' trousers, shirts and skinny ties. I wasn't particularly into fashion, but I do remember getting my first pair of 501s (jeans). They cost quite a lot at the time - around £30 - but were worth every penny. To have 501s was to be part of the in-crowd and I really wanted to fit in.

Rebecca

I remember having a huge argument with my mother in a shoe shop. She wanted me to have cheap trainers but I wouldn't have them. I told her that if I couldn't have Nike trainers then I wouldn't have any at all. I felt like I'd rather die than be seen wearing the wrong kind.

Clothes with 'designer labels' or displaying well-known logos were in demand. They showed that the wearer had spent a lot of money on them. Children also began to want the 'right' labels or logos on their sportswear. Sometimes people bought cheap copies.

POP MUSIC

Compact discs went on sale for the first time in 1982 and gradually replaced the big vinyl records or 'LPs'. 'Personal stereos' were all the rage. Others preferred to let everyone hear their music and carried around bulky radio/cassette players known as 'ghetto blasters'.

A CD player of the 1980s.

- In 1989 15% of households had a CD player. By 1998 68% of households had one.

Michael Jackson had been a child singer in seventies family band The Jackson Five. In the eighties he was a successful solo musician who combined songs with clever dance routines. His video for his hit *Thriller* was 14 minutes long and sold many millions of copies. Singer Madonna became famous in the 1980s and so did the different 'looks' that she created.

Ebru

*Michael Jackson's feature video **Thriller** was advertised days before it was actually shown on TV, and like many others I made a point of staying in to watch it. I was a big fan. I had a picture of him printed onto the back of a pink bomber jacket.*

Rebecca

I remember walking around town with my friend, carrying a 'ghetto blaster' blaring out music by Vanilla Ice. We were wearing shellsuits (a shiny kind of tracksuit), enormous trainers, and thought we were very cool.

Dance routines and looks were now an important part of pop music. New romantic band Adam and the Ants dressed like pirates, highwaymen, or whatever suited their songs.

Culture Club were famous for singer Boy George's long braids and heavy make-up (pictured left) as well as for their pop songs.

Videos brought out to promote new singles seemed as important as the music.

WORK IN THE EIGHTIES

In the early eighties people had less money to spend and businesses such as factories had to shut down. In Northern England, Scotland and South Wales many people lost their jobs. In 1981 there were 1 million people out of work and in 1982 this figure rose to 3 million. In 1984 miners went on strike in protest against pit closures and job losses. The strike lasted almost a year, but at the end of it the miners were defeated.

At the other extreme, business boomed in the financial district, where a lot of young professional people were able to 'get rich quick'. They became known as 'yuppies', which stood for 'young urban professionals'. Many of them earned huge amounts of money which they spent on luxury lifestyles.

James

Ours was a typical southeast England middle-class family, and so the recession rather passed us by. I do remember, though, the television pictures of the miners' strike, and visiting my grandparents in Nottingham, where lots of people were collecting money on the streets for the miners' families.

TECHNOLOGY AT WORK

In the 1980s word processors were replacing the office typewriter – correcting or changing documents on a word processor was much easier. Computers also changed the way that many businesses operated. Some people lost their jobs because computers could do their work.

Fax machines were another new piece of office equipment. They could instantly send letters, documents or pictures anywhere in the world using a telephone line. In the mid-eighties mobile phones were available, but they were much bigger than the ones we have today.

Fax machines became popular in the mid-1980s.

Darren

My dad was always into new hi-tech gadgets. One day he came to the house and produced a mobile phone from his rucksack. It was massive! It had a long aerial and was so heavy that he had to hold it with both hands.

TRAVELLING

People became very concerned about the air pollution caused by car exhaust fumes. A campaign was launched to encourage people to use unleaded fuel, which was less harmful than the usual '4-star' petrol. Bicycles were a much cleaner way of getting about and more people began using them around towns and cities. Some councils encouraged this by creating bicycle lanes. In 1985 Sir Clive Sinclair invented an electric tricycle called the Sinclair C5. It was environmentally friendly but it never really caught on.

The Sinclair C5.

CARS OF THE TIME

Popular cars of the day included the Fiesta, the Escort and also the Mini Metro, which, although it was one of the less expensive cars, Princess Diana was known to drive. Some people became interested in 'classic cars' which were stylish older cars from the fifties and sixties.

E100 NWN

THEN & NOW

• In 1985 a Ford Fiesta could be bought for £4,490. Today you can buy one for £7,295.

For those with a great deal of money to spend, the Porsche 911, pictured here, was the car to have. It became a symbol of wealth and success. As a joke, people would put stickers in the windows of their much cheaper cars saying: 'My other car's a Porsche'.

James

The first car we had with electric windows and a sunroof was a Vauxhall Carlton. We used to drive mum and dad mad by constantly whizzing the back windows up and down.

THE CHANNEL TUNNEL

Since the 18th century people had been working on plans and designs for a tunnel beneath the English Channel that would enable people to travel between England and France without the perils of a sea crossing. In the 1970s investigations began into the construction of a tunnel, but were eventually abandoned. Finally, in 1986, an agreement was signed between France and Britain to build a Channel Tunnel that would provide rail links between the two countries. Digging began in 1987 and the tunnel opened in 1994.

HOLIDAYS AT HOME

The British seaside still attracted many holidaymakers but holiday camps were less popular. Many people preferred the freedom of self-catering holidays, when you rented a house or flat and provided your own food. For families it was often cheaper than staying in hotels.

James

We tended to go on self-catering holidays to the seaside, usually in Devon or Norfolk. My parents would rent a farmhouse and we would spend many days on the beach. The summers seemed to be warmer then.

Darren

Every summer the whole family would go off to Blackpool for a holiday. We'd set off together in about six cars and we'd stay in seafront hotels. We had loads of fun there and every year I couldn't wait for holiday time to come round again.

HOLIDAYS ABROAD

By the 1980s air fares had become much cheaper and so lots of people travelled abroad. Holidays in the United States became very popular, particularly in Florida where children could visit Disneyland.

Rebecca

We went to Majorca on a package holiday. The brochure showed a drawing of our hotel instead of a photograph. There were so many stories in the newspapers about people turning up at holiday hotels which were still being built that we were worried about the same thing happening to us. Luckily our hotel did exist!

Ebru

We had lots of family living in Turkey, so I would spend all my summer holidays there. In those days Turkey wasn't really a holiday destination and people here didn't seem to know anything about it. Kids at school would ask me if I was going to be riding a camel or living in a tent there, and if there really were magic carpets.

News and Events

The Royal Wedding

In July 1981 the heir to the throne, Prince Charles, married 19-year-old Lady Diana Spencer in St Paul's Cathedral. The streets of London were crammed with spectators and the wedding was watched by 700 million across the world.

The Royal Wedding

THE MARRIAGE OF
The Prince of Wales
AND
Lady Diana Spencer
AT ST. PAUL'S CATHEDRAL
29 July 1981

POST OFFICE FIRST DAY COVER

Darren
I watched the royal wedding and thought that it was beautiful. I hoped that one day I'd get married in a big place like they did.

Two royal weddings were celebrated in the 1980s: that of Prince Charles and Lady Diana Spencer in 1981, then that of Prince Andrew and Sarah Ferguson in 1986.

The country celebrated and for many the glamour was a welcome escape from gloomy times. The new princess was very popular and she was always in the news.

Mrs Thatcher

The leader of the Conservative party, Margaret Thatcher, became Britain's first woman prime minister in 1979. She remained prime minister throughout the 1980s, winning three elections in a row. Because of her tough style of leadership she became known as 'the Iron Lady'.

JOHN LENNON SHOT

In December 1980 musician John Lennon was shot dead outside his home in New York by an obsessive fan. Lennon had been a member of the Beatles, the world-famous British pop band of the 1960s. The Beatles disbanded in 1970.

THE FALKLANDS WAR

In April 1982 Argentine troops invaded the Falkland Islands, a little group of British-ruled islands in the South Atlantic. Argentina had claimed that they owned the Falklands for many years, but this invasion was unexpected. British troops arrived there in May and by mid-June they had regained control. The war was short but cost Britain about £1.6 billion and over 1,000 people died. In Britain the war aroused feelings of national pride in many people and disgust in some.

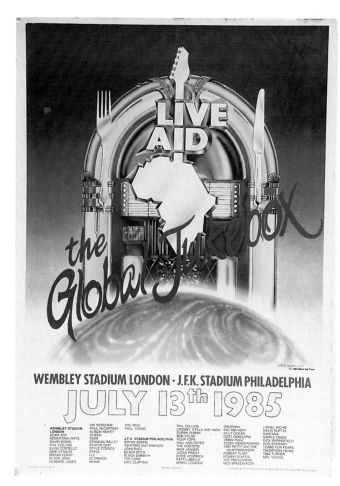

LIVE AID

In 1984 there was a terrible famine in the East African country of Ethiopia. Pop singer Bob Geldof decided to do something about it, so he persuaded top rock stars to appear in a massive charity concert. In July 1985 the 17-hour-long 'Live Aid' concert was held in London and in Philadelphia, USA, at the same time. 1.5 billion people watched it all around the world. Between performances, heartbreaking film of the dying persuaded millions to give money.

Live Aid raised over £40 million for famine relief.

WORST STORM FOR OVER 250 YEARS

In October 1987 southern England was hit by winds travelling at 115 miles per hour. Nineteen people died in the storm and it caused massive amounts of damage to property. Millions of trees were brought down, many of them blocking roads and railways.

James

The hurricane hit our town very hard. That night was very frightening and we all slept downstairs for safety. Many of our friends' houses were badly damaged and school was shut for several days.

FURTHER READING

1980s, Nicola Barber, Evans Brothers, 1993.

A Look at Life in the Eighties, Adrian Gilbert, Wayland, 1999

Take Ten Years - *1980s*, Clint Twist, Evans, 1992

20th Century Fashion - *The 80s & 90s*, Clare Lomas, Heinemann, 1999.

We Were There - *The 1980s*, Rosemary Rees, Heinemann, 1993

GLOSSARY

aerobics: A form of exercise that helps strengthen the heart and lungs as well as improve muscle tone.

breakdancing: An energetic type of street dancing that involves some gymnastic movements.

classic car: A stylish car of the fifties or sixties.

corporal punishment: A physical form of punishment such as caning.

cramming: Intensive studying during the weeks before an exam.

designer label: A fashion item designed by and carrying the name of a well-known designer.

environmentally friendly: Something that is not harmful to the environment.

logo: A design consisting of a picture or letters that a company uses as its symbol.

National Curriculum: The course of study laid down by the government and followed by schools in England and Wales.

natural resources: Materials that occur naturally in the environment and can be exploited by people, such as wood, oil or coal.

new romantic: An early eighties fashion for dressing in flamboyant and exotic clothes, often in the style of romantic characters such as pirates.

package holiday: A holiday at a set price that includes travel, accommodation and sometimes meals.

power dressing: A fashion amongst eighties businesspeople for dressing in smart, expensive outfits to make themselves look successful and businesslike.

recycling: Treating waste material, such as paper, plastic or glass, so that it can be reused. This helps to protect natural resources and also to prevent damage to the environment caused by waste disposal.

self-catering holiday: A holiday offering accommodation with facilities for preparing your own food.

shellsuit: A kind of lightweight tracksuit, often made of a slightly shiny fabric.

yuppy: A young, ambitious city worker. The word is a shortened form of 'young urban professional' or 'young upwardly-mobile professional'.

INDEX